The Essential

# Homeschool Preschool and Pre-K

## Workbook

135 Fun Curriculum-Based Activities to Build Pre-Reading, Pre-Writing, and Early Math Skills!

**Hayley Lewallen**

Illustrations by Collaborate Agency

**ROCKRIDGE PRESS**

# This Book Belongs To:

_____

To my first student, Beau.

Series Designer: Lisa Schreiber
Cover and Interior Designer: Lisa Schreiber
Art Producer: Meg Baggott
Editor: Laura Apperson
Production Editor: Nora Milman
Production Manager: Martin Worthington

Illustrations © 2021 Collaborate Agency
Author photo by Lacey Hinson

Paperback ISBN: 978-1-64876-340-3
R0

# Contents

## Easy as ABC and 123!

## Part 1: Pre-Reading Skills

### Letter Recognition

## Phonics

## Language

# Part 2: Pre-Writing Skills

## Writing Letters

## Writing Shapes and Numbers

# Part 3: Early Math Skills

## Numbers and Counting

## Early Math Skills

# Note to Homeschooling Parents

This workbook is designed for children aged 4 to 5 as a supplemental resource to your child's pre-K curriculum.

**Part 1: Pre-Reading:** These activities set the foundation for learning to read, focusing on letters, sight words, and vocabulary.

**Part 2: Pre-Writing:** In this section, we focus on fine motor skills that your child needs to be a writer. They will practice tracing and writing letters, numbers, and shapes.

**Part 3: Early Math:** These activities will work on numbers, counting, shapes, patterns, and more!

As an early childhood educator and parent myself, I have LOVED creating the activities for this workbook. My own 4-year-old son played the role of "sample student" as I developed activities.

A FEW TIPS:

→ I find it important for children to focus on one activity/skill at a time, so they do not feel overwhelmed. Please allow your child to work at their own pace.
→ YOU are their biggest cheerleader and support system. If they see you are impressed with their accomplishments in this workbook, their increased confidence will be a reflection of that.
→ You will be reading the directions and any sentences on each page to your child. For the sight word activities, do not encourage your child to "sound out" the words. These are words that they will need to recognize by sight only!
→ You will see a lot of directions that include "Point and say its name." This encourages the child to practice their speech and language skills.
→ When telling your child the sound that each letter makes, remember that most letters make quick sounds. Try not to add extra vowel sounds at the end of each letter's sound. For example, instead of "tuh" for the letter Tt, the sound should be a quick /t/ with air between your teeth.

Now let's get started!
Hayley Lewallen

# Exercise Checklist

The following checklist provides a handy way for you to keep track of the activities your child has completed.

**LETTER INTRODUCTION**

☐ Letters A to Z

**NUMBER INTRODUCTION**

☐ Numbers 0 to 10

**SHAPES AND COLORS INTRODUCTION**

☐ Shapes and Colors

**LETTER RECOGNITION**

☐ Astronaut's Adventure
☐ Bear's Balloons
☐ Candy Collection
☐ Doll Dash!
☐ Enrique's Eggs
☐ Fish Friends
☐ Can You Guess?
☐ Horse Is Hungry!
☐ Ingrid Iguana's Insects
☐ Jellybean Jars
☐ Karl's Kites
☐ Lion's Lemonade
☐ Mm Mystery
☐ Nina's Net
☐ Oscar the Octopus

☐ Pepperoni Pizza
☐ Queen's Quilt
☐ Rainy Rr's
☐ Silly Socks
☐ Turtle's Trail
☐ Under the Umbrellas
☐ Letter Volcano
☐ Walrus's Watermelon
☐ X-Ray Letters
☐ Match the Yarn
☐ Zebra's Zoo
☐ Make a Catch!
☐ Letter Match!
☐ You Did It!

**LETTER SOUNDS**

☐ Aa Is for Apple
☐ Beau's Toys
☐ Colorful Cc's
☐ Dog's Bone
☐ Exciting Eggs
☐ Frog's Friends
☐ Gum Machine
☐ Horses Love Hay
☐ Ii Items
☐ Jeep in the Jungle
☐ Katarina's Keyboard
☐ Lots of Ll's
☐ Monkey's Mess
☐ Not N!
☐ O Is for Octopus

☐ Pig's Produce
☐ Queen's Quick Quiz
☐ Rabbit's Race
☐ Starry Sounds
☐ Tons of T Words
☐ U Is for Umbrella
☐ Violet's Van
☐ Walking Whit
☐ Xx Examination
☐ Yellow Y Words
☐ Word Zap

**SIGHT WORDS**

☐ Sight Word Stars
☐ Sweet Treats
☐ Rainy Day Words
☐ Sight Word Sentences

**VOCABULARY**

☐ Match the Opposites
☐ Find the Opposite
☐ Which Is Different?
☐ Spot the Differences
☐ Weather Wear
☐ Match the Mama

**FINE MOTOR SKILLS**

☐ Writing Aa
☐ Writing Bb
☐ Writing Cc
☐ Writing Dd
☐ Writing Ee

- ☐ Writing Ff
- ☐ Writing Gg
- ☐ Writing Hh
- ☐ Writing Ii
- ☐ Writing Jj
- ☐ Writing Kk
- ☐ Writing Ll
- ☐ Writing Mm
- ☐ Writing Nn
- ☐ Writing Oo
- ☐ Writing Pp
- ☐ Writing Qq
- ☐ Writing Rr
- ☐ Writing Ss
- ☐ Writing Tt
- ☐ Writing Uu
- ☐ Writing Vv
- ☐ Writing Ww
- ☐ Writing Xx
- ☐ Writing Yy
- ☐ Writing Zz
- ☐ Let's Write Your Name!
- ☐ Shape Trace
- ☐ Writing 0
- ☐ Writing 1
- ☐ Writing 2
- ☐ Writing 3
- ☐ Writing 4
- ☐ Writing 5
- ☐ Writing 6

- ☐ Writing 7
- ☐ Writing 8
- ☐ Writing 9
- ☐ Writing 10

## NUMBER RECOGNITION

- ☐ Number 0
- ☐ Number 1
- ☐ Number 2
- ☐ Number 3
- ☐ Number 4
- ☐ Number 5
- ☐ Number 6
- ☐ Number 7
- ☐ Number 8
- ☐ Number 9
- ☐ Number 10

## COUNTING 1 TO 10

- ☐ Counting 1 to 5
- ☐ Counting 6 to 10

## SHAPES

- ☐ Spot the Shapes

## COLORS

- ☐ Yummy Colors

## PATTERNS

- ☐ Shape Pattern
- ☐ What Comes Next?
- ☐ Make Your Own Pattern!

- ☐ Missing Fruit

## SORTING AND CATEGORIZATION

- ☐ School Supplies or Lunch?
- ☐ Odd One Out
- ☐ Matching Socks
- ☐ Animal Homes

## MATCHING

- ☐ Animal Food
- ☐ Make a Match

## SIZES

- ☐ Size Them Up
- ☐ Size Match

## MEASUREMENT

- ☐ Which Holds More?
- ☐ Which Is Less?

## WEIGHT

- ☐ Which Is Heavier?
- ☐ Which Is Lighter?

# Letters A to Z

These are the letters of the alphabet! Do you know how to say your ABCs?

➡ Point to each letter of the alphabet. Say its name.

Mm Nn Oo

Pp Qq Rr

Ss Tt Uu

Vv Ww Xx

Yy Zz

# Numbers 0 to 10

These are numbers 0 to 10! Let's practice counting from 0 to 10.

➡ Point to each number. Say its name. Then count the objects that go with each number.

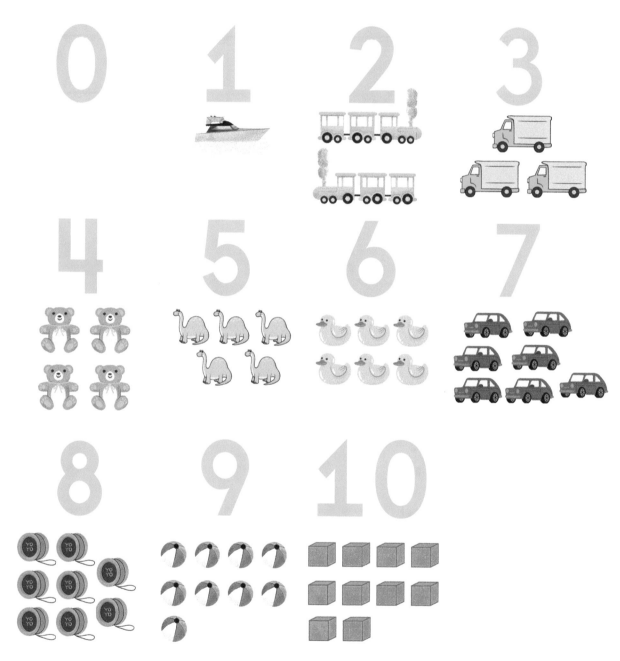

# Shapes and Colors

Shapes and colors are all around us. Let's practice saying our shapes and colors.

➡ Point to each shape. Say its name and color.

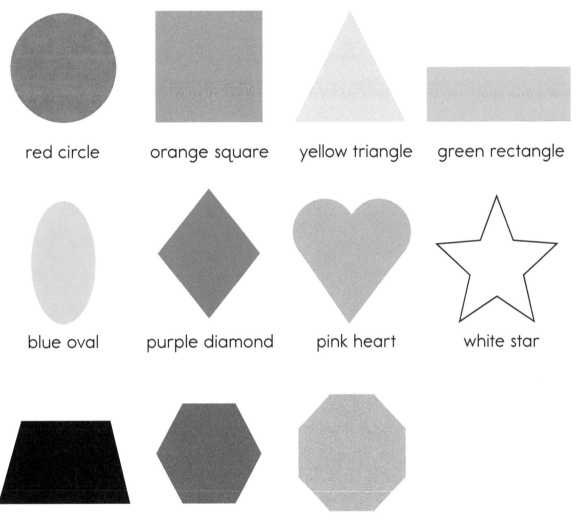

red circle    orange square    yellow triangle    green rectangle

blue oval    purple diamond    pink heart    white star

black trapezoid    brown hexagon    gray octagon

# PART 1
## Pre-Reading Skills

# 1. Astronaut's Adventure

This is the letter Aa! Touch each letter and say its name.

➡ Can you help the astronaut find his way to his spaceship? Draw a line through the letter Aa's to take him on an adventure!

**Skill:** Letter Recognition

## 2. Bear's Balloons

This is the letter Bb! Touch each letter and say its name.
Bear loves blue balloons!

➡ Can you color all the balloons with Bb's on them blue?
Put an X on the balloons that do not have the letter Bb.

# 3. Candy Collection

This is the letter Cc! Touch each letter and say its name.

➡ Do you like candy? It's so yummy! Find and circle all the pieces of candy with the letter Cc on them!

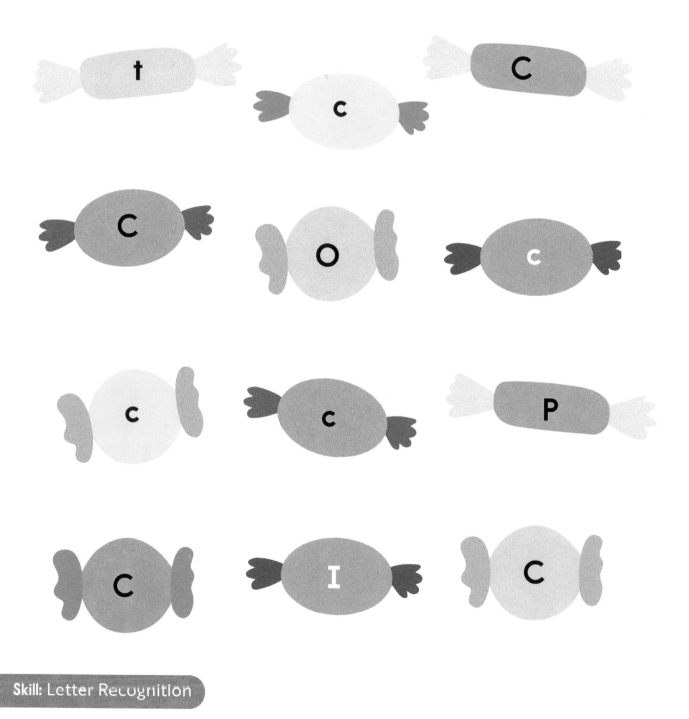

**Skill:** Letter Recognition

# 4. Doll Dash!

This is the letter Dd! Touch each letter and say its name.

➡ Quick! It's time to put away the dolls! Can you draw a line to match each doll to the correct toy box?

# 5. Enrique's Eggs

**E e**

This is the letter Ee! Touch each letter and say its name.
➡ Can you help Enrique find all the letter Ee eggs? Circle each egg that you find!

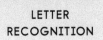
# 6. Fish Friends

This is the letter Ff! Touch each letter and say its name.

➡ The fish are looking for their friends! Draw a line to match each fish to the correct fish tank.

# 7. Can You Guess?

**Gg**

This is the letter Gg! Touch each letter and say its name.

➡ Can you guess what is hidden in the picture? Color the letter Gg's to reveal a surprise!

G = ▮ g = ▯

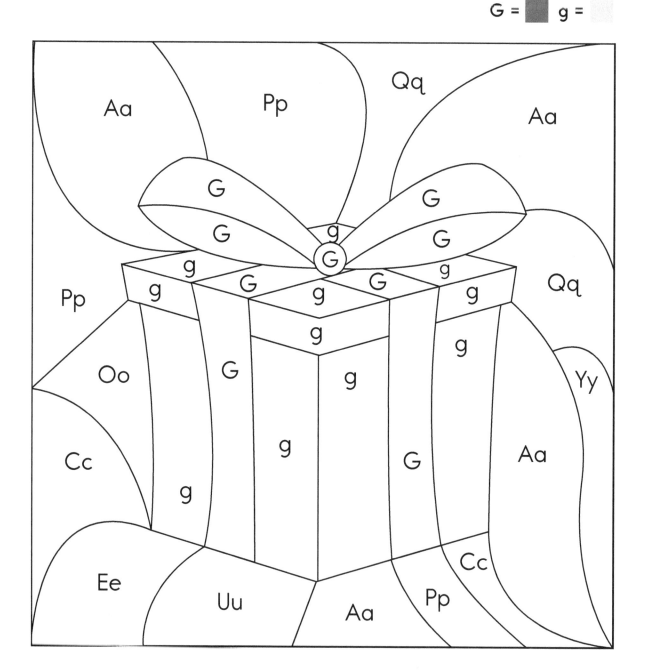

# 8. Horse Is Hungry!

This is the letter Hh! Touch each letter and say its name.
➡ The horse is very hungry. Can you help her get to her hay by coloring in all the letter Hh's and showing her the path?

| Hh | Gg | Aa | Yy | Ii | Uu | Ff |
|----|----|----|----|----|----|----|
| Hh | Hh | Hh | Bb | Hh | Hh | Hh |
| Nn | Yy | Hh | Xx | Hh | Ee | Hh |
| Mm | Ii | Hh | Hh | Hh | Jj | Hh |
| Aa | Uu | Ff | Gg | Hh | Hh | Hh |
| Bb | Rr | Ww | Ee | Hh | Mm | Yy |
| Jj | Qq | Nn | Ff | Hh | Hh | Hh |

**Skill:** Letter Recognition

# 9. Ingrid Iguana's Insects

## Ii

This is the letter Ii! Touch each letter and say its name.

➡ Ingrid Iguana needs to catch the Ii insects! Circle all the insects with the letter Ii on them!

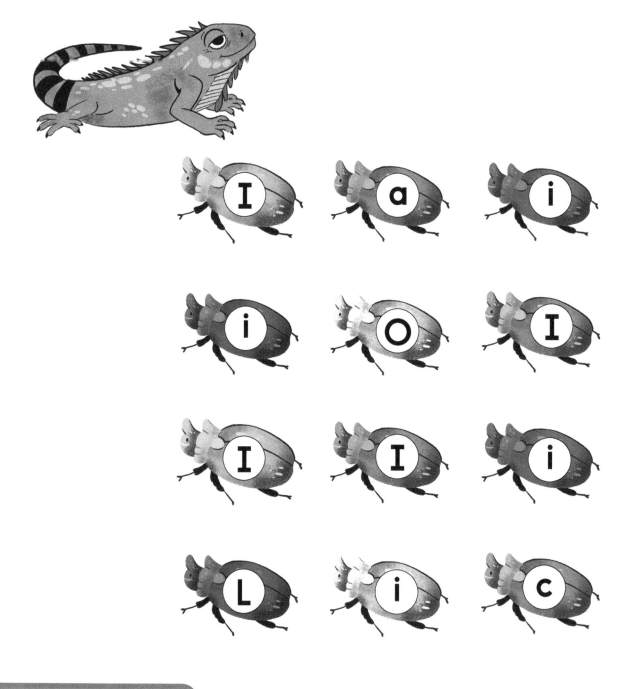

# 10. Jellybean Jars

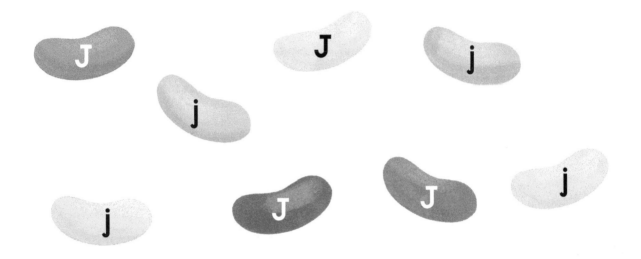

This is the letter Jj! Touch each letter and say its name.
➡ The jelly beans are all mixed up! Can you sort them out?
Draw a line from each jelly bean to the correct jar.

# 11. Karl's Kites

This is the letter Kk! Touch each letter and say its name.
➡ Karl has lost his kites! Help Karl find all his kites. Circle each Kk kite you see.

# 12. Lion's Lemonade

**Ll**

This is the letter Ll! Touch each letter and say its name.

➡ Lion is making lemonade with letter Ll lemons. Circle all the lemons with the letter Ll.

## 13. Mm Mystery

**Mm** This is the letter Mm! Touch each letter and say its name.

➡ There's a mystery to solve! What will the letter Mm's reveal? Color all the Mm's to find out!

Mm =

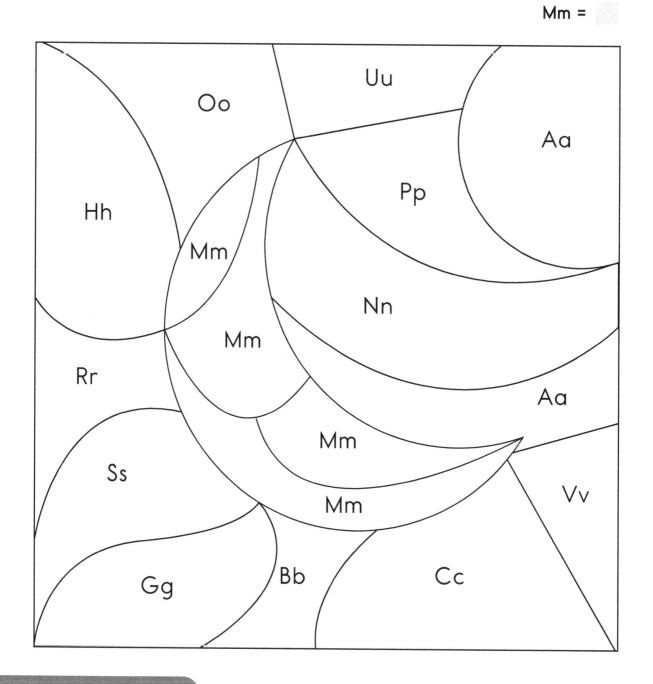

# 14. Nina's Net

This is the letter Nn! Touch each letter and say its name.

➡ Nina needs help catching all the Nn's! Circle all the Nn's in the water.

# 15. Oscar the Octopus

This is the letter Oo! Touch each letter and say its name.
➡ Oscar the octopus wants to return to his reef. Help Oscar find his way back by drawing a line through the letter Oo's.

# 16. Pepperoni Pizza

**Pp**

This is the letter Pp! Touch each letter and say its name.

➡ It's time to make pizza! Draw a line from each Pp pepperoni to the pizza.

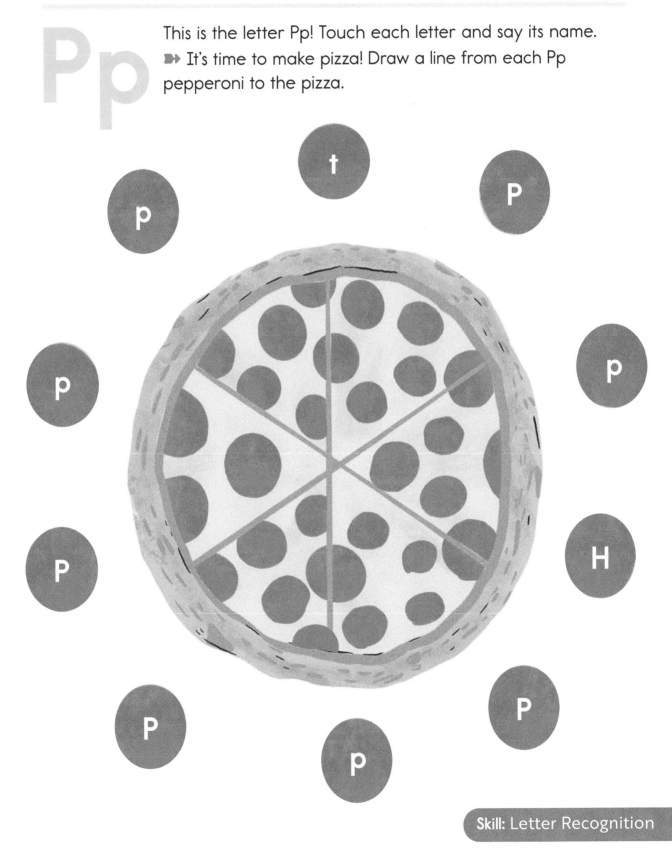

# 17. Queen's Quilt

This is the letter Qq! Touch each letter and say its name.

➡ The queen wants a colorful quilt. Color the Qq's using the color code below.

Q = ⬛  q = ⬜

# 18. Rainy Rr's

Rr

This is the letter Rr! Touch each letter and say its name.

➡ It's a rainy day! Find and circle all the raindrops with the letter Rr.

## 19. Silly Socks

**S s** This is the letter Ss! Touch each letter and say its name.
➡ The socks are all mixed up! Draw a line from each sock to its matching basket.

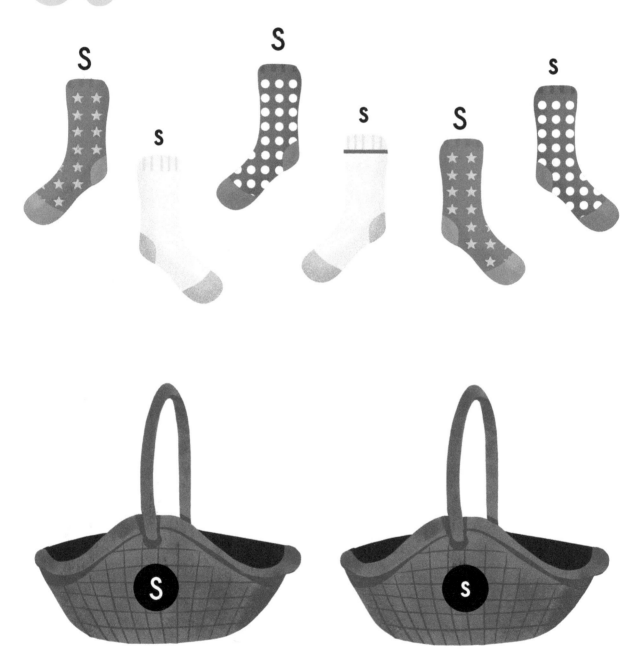

# 20. Turtle's Trail

**T t** This is the letter Tt! Touch each letter and say its name.

➡ Turtle is going for a walk. Can you spot all the hidden Tt's along the trail? Circle each Tt you see.

# 21. Under the Umbrellas

**Uu**

This is the letter Uu! Touch each letter and say its name.
➡ Can you find all the letter Uu umbrellas? Color each one you find. Put an X on the umbrellas that do not have a U.

# 22. Letter Volcano

**Vv** This is the letter Vv! Touch each letter and say its name.
➡ The volcano is erupting letters! Find and circle all the Vv's you see.

# 23. Walrus's Watermelon

This is the letter Ww! Touch each letter and say its name.

➡ Walrus is hungry and wants his watermelon! Help walrus get to his snack by coloring in the letter Ww's.

| Ww | Ee | Uu | Jj | Oo | Rr | Ss |
|----|----|----|----|----|----|----|
| Ww | Qq | Zz | Cc | Rr | Ee | Ii |
| Ww | Kk | Ll | Nn | Mm | Bb | Vv |
| Ww | Ww | Ww | Yy | Aa | Tt | Cc |
| Ii | Oo | Ww | Gg | Gg | Ee | Qq |
| Dd | Ff | Ww | Ww | Ww | Ww | Yy |
| Ll | Yy | Nn | Gg | Bb | Ww | Ww |

# 24. X-Ray Letters

This is the letter Xx! Touch each letter and say its name.

➡ Time to examine the X-rays! Circle all the X-rays with the letter Xx.

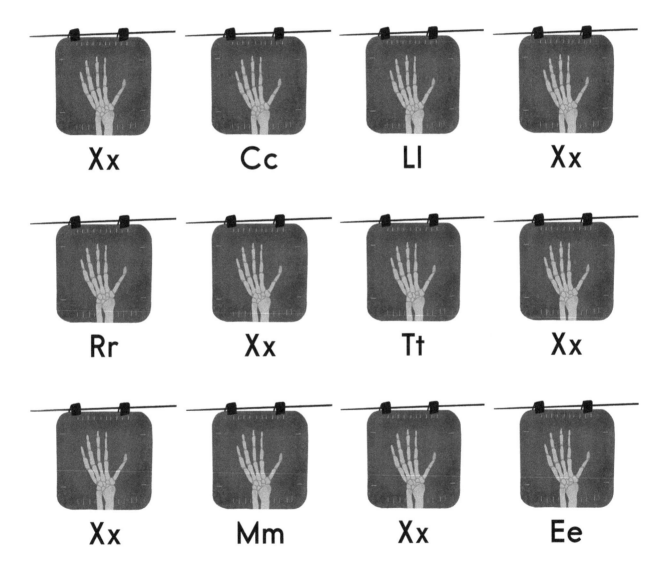

| Xx | Cc | Ll | Xx |
| Rr | Xx | Tt | Xx |
| Xx | Mm | Xx | Ee |

**Skill:** Letter Recognition

# 25. Match the Yarn

**Yy**

This is the letter Yy! Touch each letter and say its name.
➡ The yarn is all mixed up. Draw a line from each ball of yarn to the correct basket.

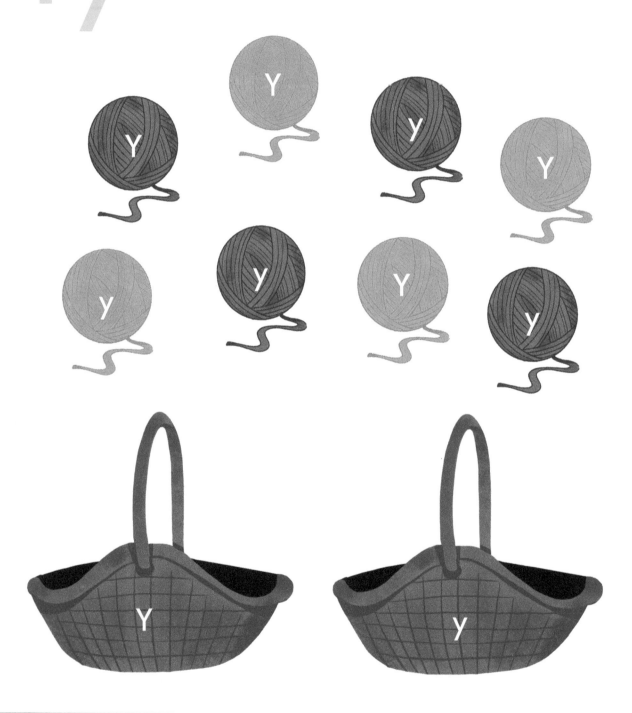

## 26. Zebra's Zoo

This is the letter Zz! Touch each letter and say its name.

➡ Zebra is looking for Zz's! Help zebra find all the hidden Zz's at the zoo.

**Skill:** Letter Recognition

# 27. Make a Catch!

Wow! You are rocking these activities! Let's review some of our letters.
➡ Draw a line to match each lowercase letter ball to the correct uppercase letter glove.

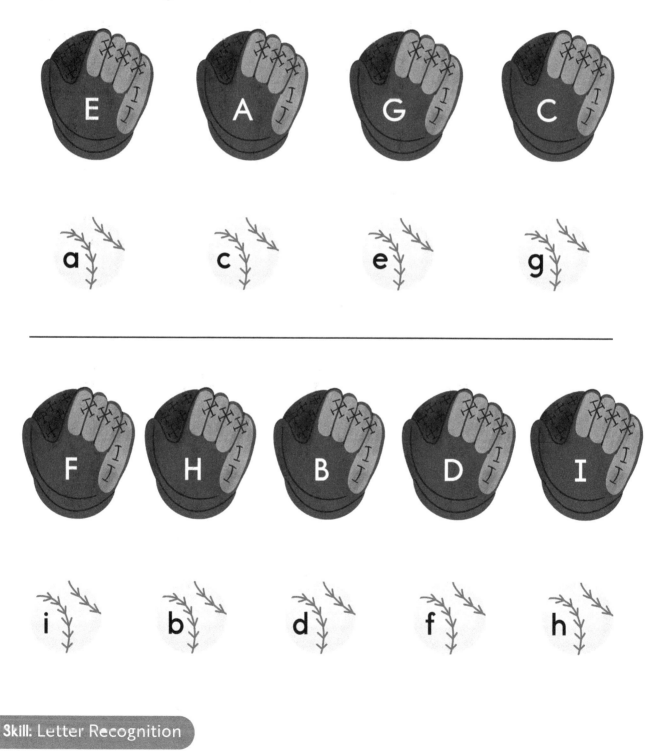

# 28. Letter Match!

Awesome! Way to go! Let's review some more letters.
➡ For each row, color the lowercase letter that matches the uppercase letter in the pink heart.

# 29. You Did It!

Great job! You've made it through all the letter recognition activities!
➡ You have been working so hard. It's time for you to earn your prize!
Starting with the letter T, connect each uppercase letter to its lowercase
letter. Then go on to the next uppercase letter in the alphabet, making the
final connection back to the T. Color in your prize when you're finished!

# 30. Aa Is for Apple

A is a vowel. That means it has two sounds!

A says /ă/ like apple! Pretend you're eating an APPLE. You open your mouth big and wide to take a bite. This is what your mouth looks like when you say the /ă/ sound. Point to the picture and say the word!

A also says /ā/ (long a sound) like ACORN. Vowels can say their own name in words! Point to the picture and say the word!

Point to each letter and say the /ă/ sound. Now point to each letter and say the /ā/ sound.

➡ Point to each picture below and say its name. Draw a line from Aa to the words that start with the A sounds like in apple and acorn.

# 31. Beau's Toys

**Bb** B says /b/ like you hear at the beginning of ball. Put your lips together as you get ready to say BALL. Point to the picture and say the word!

Point to each letter and say the /b/ sound.

➥ Beau needs help cleaning up! Point to each toy and say its name. Circle all the toys that start with the B sound like ball.

# 32. Colorful Cc's

C says /c/ like you hear at the beginning of candy. Open your mouth as you get ready to say CANDY. Point to the picture and say the word! Do you hear how the /c/ sound comes from the back of your mouth?

Point to each letter and say the /c/ sound.

➡ Let's color some pictures! Point to each picture and say its name. If it starts with the C sound, color it!

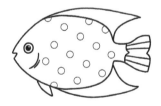

**Skill:** Letter Sounds

# 33. Dog's Bone

D says /d/ like you hear at the beginning of dog. Put your tongue behind your top teeth as you get ready to say DOG. Point to the picture and say the word! Do you feel your tongue move as you say the word dog?

Point to each letter and say the /d/ sound.

➡ The dog buried her bone. Now she can't find it! Draw lines to connect the pictures that begin with the D sound to help the dog find her bone.

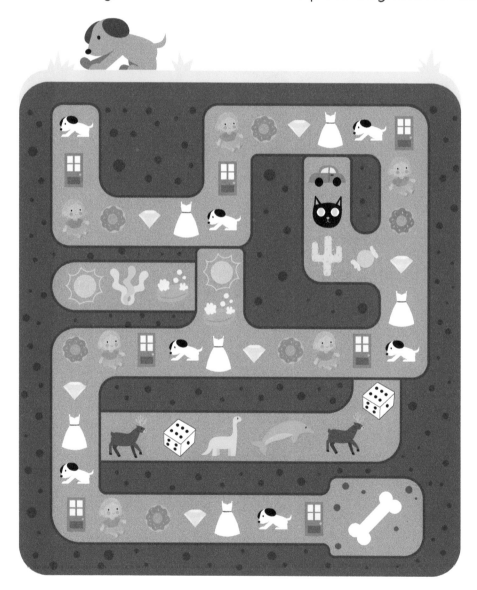

**Skill: Letter Sounds**

# 34. Exciting Eggs

E is a vowel. That means it has two sounds!

E says /ĕ/ like egg! Put your pointer fingers on the corners of your mouth. As you open your mouth to say EGG, you will feel the corners of your mouth push back when you say the /ĕ/ sound. Point to the picture and say the word!

E also says /ē/ (long e sound) like easel! Vowels can say their own name in words! Point to the picture and say the word!

Point to each letter and say the /ĕ/ sound. Now point to each letter and say the /ē/ sound.

➡ Point to the picture on each egg and say its name. Color the pictures that start with the E sounds that you hear at the beginning of egg and easel. If it does not start with E, put an X on it.

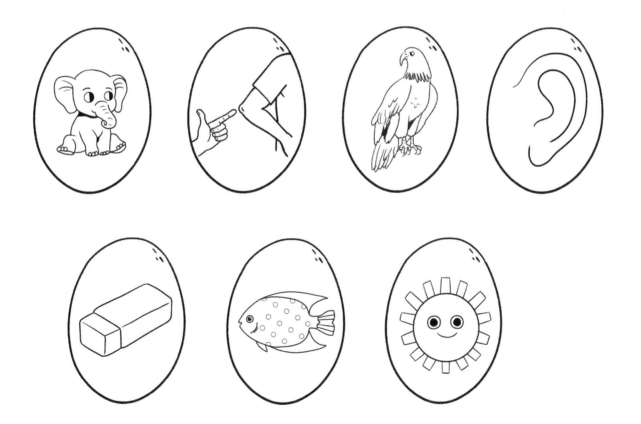

# 35. Frog's Friends

 F says /f/ like in frog! Put your top teeth on your bottom lip. As you get ready to say FROG, you will feel the air come out under your teeth as you say the /f/ sound. Point to the picture and say the word!

Point to each letter and say the /f/ sound.

➡ Help the frog find his friends that start with the F sound. Point to each animal and say its name. Draw a line from the frog to the animals that start with the F sound.

**Skill:** Letter Sounds

# 36. Gum Machine

G says /g/ like glasses! Get ready to say GLASSES. As you open your mouth, you'll feel the /g/ sound come from the back of your mouth. Point to the picture and say the word!

Point to each letter and say the /g/ sound.

➡ Point to each picture in the gum machine and say its name. Circle the pictures that start with the G sound like in gum.

# 37. Horses Love Hay

Hh  H says /h/ like horse! Get ready to say HORSE. As you open your mouth, you'll feel your breath come from the back of your mouth to make the /h/ sound. Point to the picture and say the word!

Point to each letter and say the /h/ sound.

➡ Did you know horses love to eat hay? Look at the picture and circle all the items that start with H like in horse.

**Skill:** Letter Sounds

# 38. Ii Items

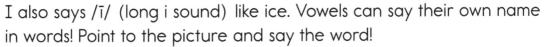

**Ii** I is a vowel. That means it has two sounds!

I says /ĭ/ like insect! Put your pointer finger on the tip of your nose. As you get ready to say INSECT, gently push up on your nose as you say the /ĭ/ sound. Point to the picture and say the word!

I also says /ī/ (long i sound) like ice. Vowels can say their own name in words! Point to the picture and say the word!

Point to each letter and say the /ĭ/ sound. Now point to each letter and say the /ī/ sound.

➡ Point to each picture and say its name. If it starts with an I sound, draw a line to the letter I. If it does not start with an I sound, draw a line to the I with an X on it.

# 39. Jeep in the Jungle

J says /j/ like jeep! Get ready to say JEEP. As you open your mouth, you'll feel your tongue come away from the roof of your mouth to make the /j/ sound. Point to the picture and say the word! Point to each letter and say the /j/ sound.

➡ The jeep is lost in the jungle! Help the jeep find its way out. Draw lines to connect the pictures that start with the J sound.

**Skill:** Letter Sounds

# 40. Katarina's Keyboard

K says /k/ like kite! Get ready to say KITE. As you open your mouth, you'll feel the /k/ sound come from the back of your mouth. Point to the picture and say the word!

Point to each letter and say the /k/ sound.

➡ Katarina is looking for K pictures on her keyboard! Find and circle all the pictures on the keyboard that start with the K sound like in kite.

**Skill:** Letter Sounds

# 41. Lots of Ll's

 L says /l/ like lion! Get ready to say LION. You will feel your tongue touch the roof of your mouth behind your top teeth. Point to the picture and say the word!

Point to each letter and say the /l/ sound.

➡ The letter Ll is in a LOT of words! Point to each picture and say its name. Color all the spaces with pictures that start with the L sound like in lion. What did you find?

# 42. Monkey's Mess

M says /m/ like monkey! Get ready to say MONKEY. Put your lips together and make the /m/ sound before you open your mouth. Point to the picture and say the word!

Point to each letter and say the /m/ sound.

➡ Monkey has a mess in her tree! Can you help her clean it up? Circle all the pictures that start with the M sound.

**Skill:** Letter Sounds

# 43. Not N!

N says /n/ like nest! Get ready to say NEST. You will feel your tongue touch the roof of your mouth behind your top teeth. Point to the picture and say the word!

Point to each letter and say the /n/ sound.

➡ Point to each picture and say its name. Each box has a picture of something that starts with the N sound and a picture of something that does NOT start with the N sound. Put an X on each picture that does NOT start with N.

**Skill:** Letter Sounds

# 44. O Is for Octopus

O is a vowel. That means it has two sounds!

O says /ŏ/ like OCTOPUS! Open your mouth big and wide like you are going to sing opera! Point to the picture and say the word!

O also says /ō/ (long o sound) like oval! Vowels can say their own name in words! Point to the picture and say the word!

Point to each letter and say the /ŏ/ sound. Now point to each letter and say the /ō/ sound.

➥ Point to picture and say its name. If it starts with an O sound, color it!

# 45. Pig's Produce

P p

P says /p/ like pig! Get ready to say PIG. Put your lips together and you will feel the air come out as you make the /p/ sound. Point to the picture and say the word!

Point to each letter and say the /p/ sound.

➡ Pig is hungry for P foods! Circle each food that starts with the P sound.

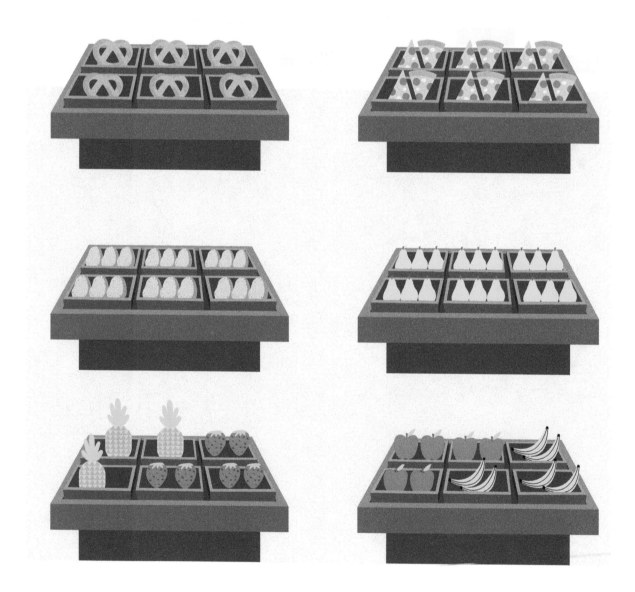

# 46. Queen's Quick Quiz

Q says /q/ like queen! Get ready to say QUEEN. Open your mouth and listen for the /q/ sound to come from the back. Point to the picture and say the word!

Point to each letter and say the /q/ sound.

➡ It's time for the queen to take a quick quiz! Help the queen find things that begin with the Q sound by putting a check mark ☑ next to the Q pictures. Put an X on the pictures that do not start with the Q sound.

**Skill:** Letter Sounds

# 47. Rabbit's Race

R says /r/ like rabbit! Get ready to say RABBIT. Open your mouth and listen for the /r/ sound to come from the back. When you say it, it will sound like you are growling! Point to the picture and say the word!

Point to each letter and say the /r/ sound.

➡ Help the rabbit reach the finish line! Draw lines to connect all the pictures that begin with the R sound.

**Skill:** Letter Sounds

# 48. Starry Sounds

**Ss** ⭐ S says /s/ like star! Get ready to say STAR. Put your teeth close together and say the /s/ sound like a snake. Point to the picture and say the word!

Point to each letter and say the /s/ sound.

➡ Point to each picture and say its name. Circle the pictures that begin with the S sound.

# 49. Tons of T Words

 **Tt**

T says /t/ like turtle! Get ready to say TURTLE. Put your teeth close together. Point to the picture and say the word!

Point to each letter and say the /t/ sound.

➡ The letter Tt is in a TON of words! Point to each picture and say its name. Color all the spaces with pictures that start with the T sound. What did you find?

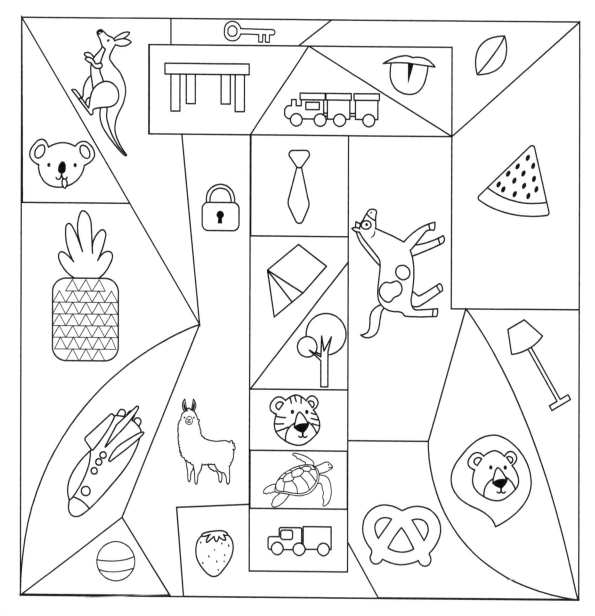

**Skill:** Letter Sounds

# 50. U Is for Umbrella

**Uu**

 U is a vowel. That means it has two sounds!

U says /ŭ/ like UMBRELLA! Open your mouth and listen for the /ŭ/ sound at the back of your throat. Point to the picture and say the word!

U also says /ū/ (long u sound) like UNICORN! Vowels can say their own name in words! Point to the picture and say the word!

Point to each letter and say the /ŭ/ sound. Now point to each letter and say the /ū/ sound.

➡ Point each picture and say its name. Color the pictures that start with the U sound.

**Skill:** Letter Sounds

# 51. Violet's Van

V says /v/ like van! Get ready to say VAN. Put your top teeth on your bottom lip and make the /v/ sound. You will feel your lip vibrate! Point to the picture and say the word!

Point to each letter and say the /v/ sound.

➡ Violet is loading her van with letter Vv objects. Point to each picture and say its name. If it starts with the V sound, draw a line from the picture to Violet's van.

# 52. Walking Whit

W says /w/ like watermelon! Get ready to say WATERMELON. Pull your lips apart as you make the /w/ sound. Point to the picture and say the word!

Point to each letter and say the /w/ sound.

➡ Whit is walking around outside. Point to each object in the picture and say its name. Circle the objects that start with the W sound.

**Skill:** Letter Sounds

# 53. Xx Examination

X says /x/ like xylophone! X is at the beginning of some words, but most of the time you will hear it at the END of words! Listen to the /x/ sound at the beginning of XYLOPHONE as you say the word. Point to the picture and say the word!

Now, listen to the /x/ sound at the END of the word fox! Point to the picture and say the word!

Point to each letter and say the /x/ sound.

➡ Point to each picture around the xylophone and say its name. If it starts with the X sound, draw a line to connect it to the xylophone.

➡ Point to each picture around the fox and say its name. If it ends with the X sound, draw a line to connect it to the fox.

# 54. Yellow Y Words

Y says /y/ like yo-yo! When you say the word YO-YO, you will feel the /y/ sound come from the back of your mouth. Point to the picture and say the word!

Point to each letter and say the /y/ sound.

➡ Yellow starts with the Y sound! Use a yellow crayon to circle the picture that starts with the Y sound in each row.

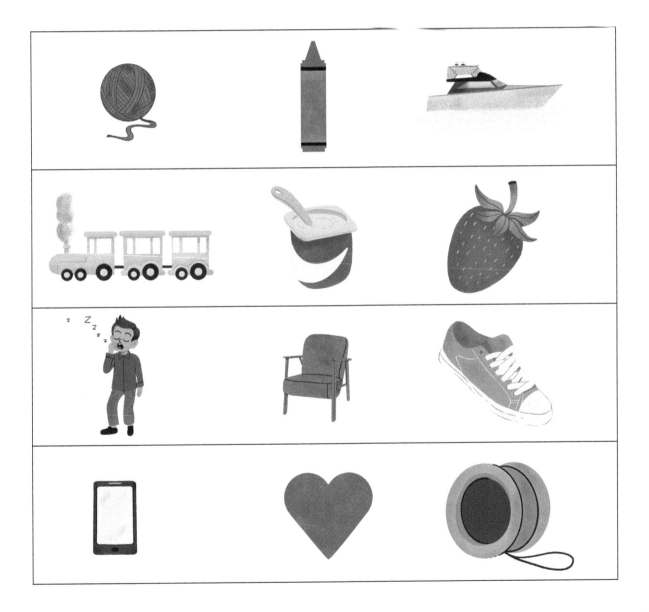

# 55. Word Zap

Z says /z/ like zebra! When you say the word ZEBRA, you will feel your teeth vibrate as you say the /z/ sound! Point to the picture and say the word!

Point to each letter and say the /z/ sound.

➡ Point to each picture and say its name. Each box has a picture of something that starts with the Z sound and a picture of something that does NOT start with the Z sound. Color the picture that starts with the Z sound. Zap out the picture that does NOT start with the Z sound by drawing an X over it.

# 56. Sight Word Stars

Sight words are words we should recognize by sight, not by sounding them out.

Point to each word as you say it.

go | see | play | we | my

➡ Read the word on each star. Use the color code to color each star.

play = ☐  we = ☐  see = ☐  go = ☐  my = ☐

# 57. Sweet Treats

Point to each word as you say it.

I | can | big | you | the | it

➡ Read the word on each ice-cream scoop. Draw a line to match the scoop with the cone that has the same sight word.

**Skill:** Sight Words

# 58. Rainy Day Words

Point to each word as you say it.

## a | is | to | look | jump

➡ Read each word in the puzzle. Color the pieces of the puzzle using the color code. You will find out what you might need on a rainy day!

a = ☐   is = ☐   to = ☐   look = ☐   jump = ☐

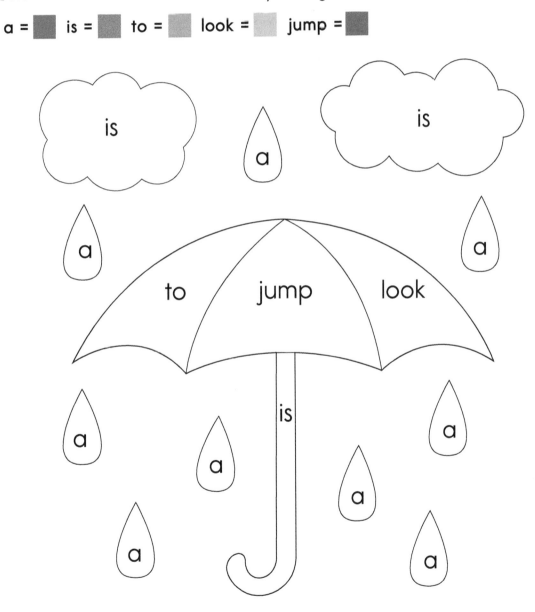

Skill: Sight Words

# 59. Sight Word Sentences

Point to each word as you say it.

## here | me | run | said

➡ Read each sentence. Circle the word that should go on the blank line.

I like to _____ (run, said).

We are _____ (me, here).

My mom _____ (here, said)
I am four.

This apple is for _____ (me, run).

# 60. Match the Opposites

➡ Look at each picture. Draw a line to match each picture with its opposite.

**soft**

**night**

**young**

**sad**

**happy**

**hard**

**day**

**old**

# 61. Find the Opposite

➡ Look at each picture on the left. Circle the picture on the right that shows its opposite.

# 62. Which Is Different?

➡ Look at each row of fruit. Circle the fruit that is different from the others.

# 63. Spot the Differences

➡ Look at the two pictures. Find and circle five differences.

# 64. Weather Wear

There are four seasons in a year. The seasons are winter, spring, summer, and fall. Each season brings different weather.

➡ Look at the pictures of the different weather. Draw a line from each picture to the child who is wearing the correct clothes for that weather.

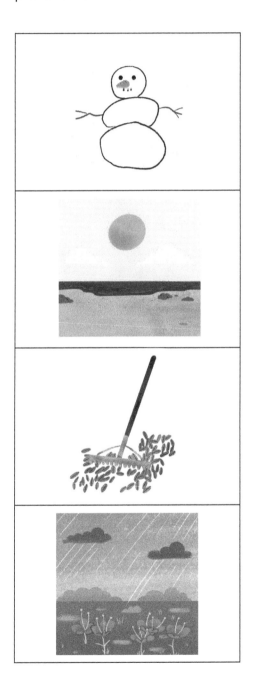

# 65. Match the Mama

Some animal babies look different from their mothers.

➡ Draw a line to match each animal baby with its mother.

# PART 2
## Pre-Writing Skills

# 1. Writing Aa

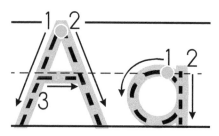

➥ Trace each letter. Use the dot as the starting point and follow the arrows to form the letter.

➥ Read the sentence to your child. Point to each word as you read it. Have your child trace the letter to spell the word in the picture.

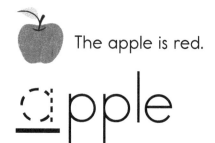
The apple is red.

apple

I have one acorn.

acorn

**Skill: Fine Motor Skills**

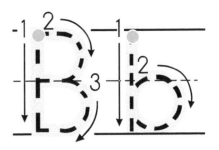

# 2. Writing Bb

➡ Trace each letter. Use the dot as the starting point and follow the arrows to form the letter.

➡ Read the sentence to your child. Point to each word as you read it. Have your child trace the letter to spell the word in the picture.

I see a bear.

bear

# 3. Writing Cc

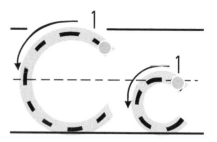

➡ Trace each letter. Use the dot as the starting point and follow the arrows to form the letter.

➡ Read the sentence to your child. Point to each word as you read it. Have your child trace the letter to spell the word in the picture.

I like to eat candy!

candy

# 4. Writing Dd

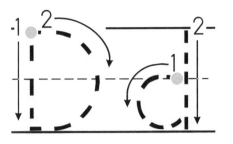

➤ Trace each letter. Use the dot as the starting point and follow the arrows to form the letter.

➤ Read the sentence to your child. Point to each word as you read it. Have your child trace the letter to spell the word in the picture.

Ducks can swim and fly.

duck

# 5. Writing Ee

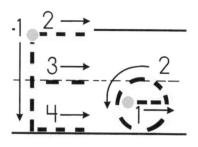

➤ Trace each letter. Use the dot as the starting point and follow the arrows to form the letter.

➤ Read the sentence to your child. Point to each word as you read it. Have your child trace the letter to spell the word in the picture.

The elephant is
big and gray.

I like to paint on
my easel.

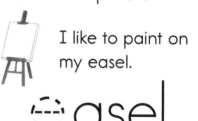

elephant

easel

# 6. Writing Ff

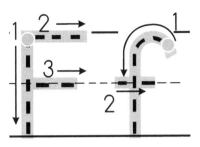

➽ Trace each letter. Use the dot as the starting point and follow the arrows to form the letter.

➽ Read the sentence to your child. Point to each word as you read it. Have your child trace the letter to spell the word in the picture.

Fish live in the water.

ish

# 7. Writing Gg

➡ Trace each letter. Use the dot as the starting point and follow the arrows to form the letter.

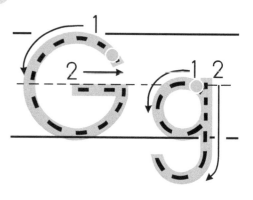

➡ Read the sentence to your child. Point to each word as you read it. Have your child trace the letter to spell the word in the picture.

I like my new glasses.

lasses

# 8. Writing Hh

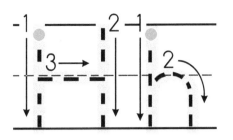

➡ Trace each letter. Use the dot as the starting point and follow the arrows to form the letter.

➡ Read the sentence to your child. Point to each word as you read it. Have your child trace the letter to spell the word in the picture.

My favorite hat is blue.

# 9. Writing Ii

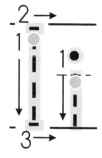

➡ Trace each letter. Use the dot as the starting point and follow the arrows to form the letter.

➡ Read the sentence to your child. Point to each word as you read it. Have your child trace the letter to spell the word in the picture.

The insect can fly.

Ice is made of water.

insect

ice

**Skill:** Fine Motor Skills

# 10. Writing Jj

➠ Trace each letter. Use the dot as the starting point and follow the arrows to form the letter.

➠ Read the sentence to your child. Point to each word as you read it. Have your child trace the letter to spell the word in the picture.

The jeep can go fast.

**Skill:** Fine Motor Skills

# 11. Writing Kk

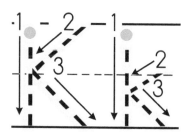

➡ Trace each letter. Use the dot as the starting point and follow the arrows to form the letter.

➡ Read the sentence to your child. Point to each word as you read it. Have your child trace the letter to spell the word in the picture.

This is the key to my house.

key

# 12. Writing Ll

➠ Trace each letter. Use the dot as the starting point and follow the arrows to form the letter.

➠ Read the sentence to your child. Point to each word as you read it. Have your child trace the letter to spell the word in the picture.

I have a green leaf.

ₗeaf

**Skill:** Fine Motor Skills

# 13. Writing Mm

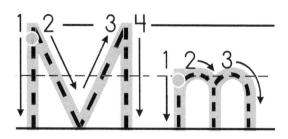

➡ Trace each letter. Use the dot as the starting point and follow the arrows to form the letter.

➡ Read the sentence to your child. Point to each word as you read it. Have your child trace the letter to spell the word in the picture.

Monkeys can swing on trees.

 onkey

# 14. Writing Nn

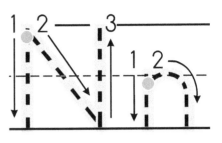

➽ Trace each letter. Use the dot as the starting point and follow the arrows to form the letter.

➽ Read the sentence to your child. Point to each word as you read it. Have your child trace the letter to spell the word in the picture.

I can smell with my nose.

nose

# 15. Writing Oo

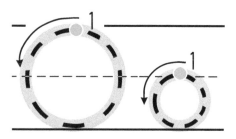

➡ Trace each letter. Use the dot as the starting point and follow the arrows to form the letter.

➡ Read the sentence to your child. Point to each word as you read it. Have your child trace the letter to spell the word in the picture.

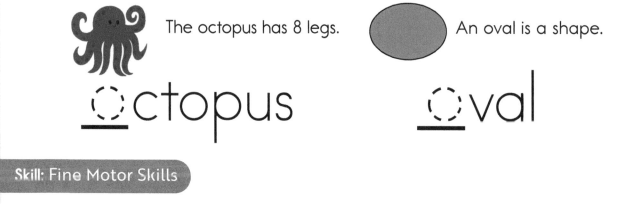

The octopus has 8 legs.

An oval is a shape.

octopus

oval

# 16. Writing Pp

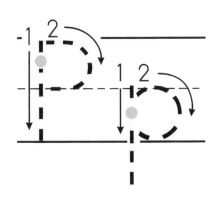

➡ Trace each letter. Use the dot as the starting point and follow the arrows to form the letter.

➡ Read the sentence to your child. Point to each word as you read it. Have your child trace the letter to spell the word in the picture.

  Pigs love to play in the mud.

# 17. Writing Qq

➡ Trace each letter. Use the dot as the starting point and follow the arrows to form the letter.

➡ Read the sentence to your child. Point to each word as you read it. Have your child trace the letter to spell the word in the picture.

The queen is wearing her crown.

**Skill: Fine Motor Skills**

# 18. Writing Rr

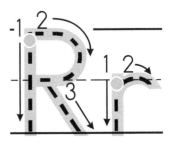

➡ Trace each letter. Use the dot as the starting point
and follow the arrows to form the letter.

➡ Read the sentence to your child. Point to each word as you read it.
Have your child trace the letter to spell the word in the picture.

The rabbit is small and fast.

rabbit

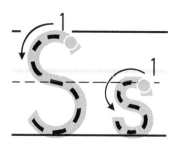

# 19. Writing Ss

➡ Trace each letter. Use the dot as the starting point and follow the arrows to form the letter.

➡ Read the sentence to your child. Point to each word as you read it. Have your child trace the letter to spell the word in the picture.

I see a star in the sky.

_Star

# 20. Writing Tt

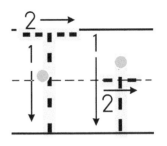

➡ Trace each letter. Use the dot as the starting point and follow the arrows to form the letter.

➡ Read the sentence to your child. Point to each word as you read it. Have your child trace the letter to spell the word in the picture.

A turtle has a shell.

turtle

# 21. Writing Uu

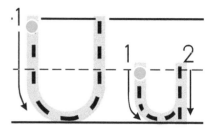

➡ Trace each letter. Use the dot as the starting point and follow the arrows to form the letter.

➡ Read the sentence to your child. Point to each word as you read it. Have your child trace the letter to spell the word in the picture.

 My umbrella is green.

Umbrella

 The unicorn is pretty!

Unicorn

# 22. Writing Vv

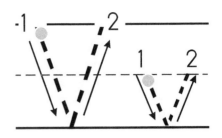

➡ Trace each letter. Use the dot as the starting point and follow the arrows to form the letter.

➡ Read the sentence to your child. Point to each word as you read it. Have your child trace the letter to spell the word in the picture.

The vase can hold flowers.

**_V**ase

# 23. Writing Ww

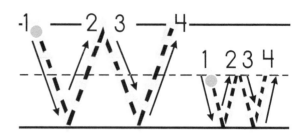

➽ Trace each letter. Use the dot as the starting point and follow the arrows to form the letter.

➽ Read the sentence to your child. Point to each word as you read it. Have your child trace the letter to spell the word in the picture.

I like to eat watermelon.

 atermelon

# 24. Writing Xx

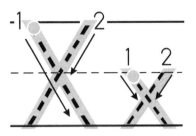

➡ Trace each letter. Use the dot as the starting point and follow the arrows to form the letter.

➡ Read the sentence to your child. Point to each word as you read it. Have your child trace the letter to spell the word in the picture.

I can play the xylophone.

xylophone

The fox is quick.

fox

**Skill:** Fine Motor Skills

# 25. Writing Yy

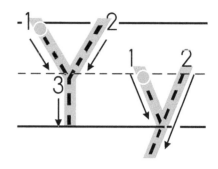

➠ Trace each letter. Use the dot as the starting point and follow the arrows to form the letter.

➠ Read the sentence to your child. Point to each word as you read it. Have your child trace the letter to spell the word in the picture.

I can spin the yo-yo.

Yo-yo

# 26. Writing Zz

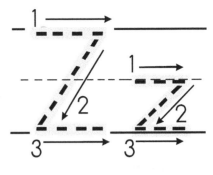

➠ Trace each letter. Use the dot as the starting point and follow the arrows to form the letter.

➠ Read the sentence to your child. Point to each word as you read it. Have your child trace the letter to spell the word in the picture.

I can zip up my jacket.

zip

# 27. Let's Write Your Name!

Did you know your name is made up of letters? Now that you have practiced writing all 26 letters, you can practice writing your own name!

➡ Look at the uppercase letters. Circle the letter at the beginning of your name.

➡ Look at the lowercase letters. Circle the letters that are in your name.

A B C D E F G H I J K L M N O P
Q R S T U V W X Y Z
a b c d e f g h i j k l m n o p q r
s t u v w x y z

➡ Let's practice writing your name!

➡ Now draw a picture of yourself!

# 28. Shape Trace

Our world is made up of many different shapes. Houses are even made of shapes!

➥ Trace the shapes to make a house. After you trace the house, color it!

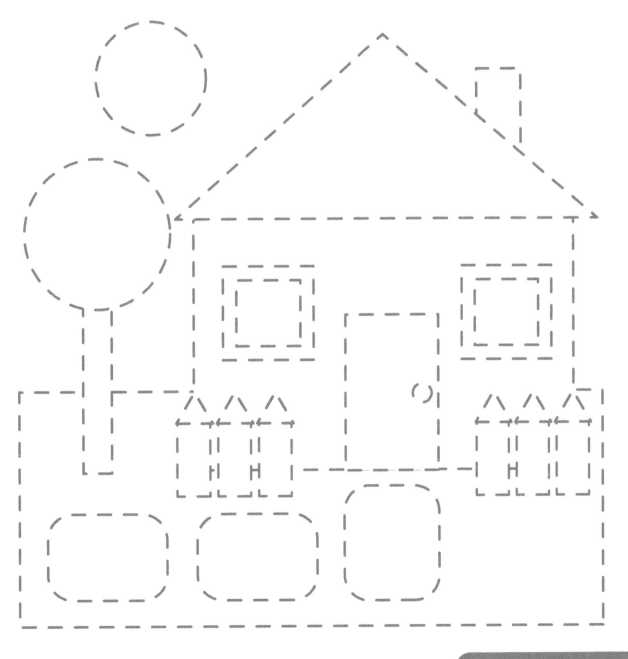

## 29. Writing 0

➡ Trace each number 0. Use the dot as the starting point and follow the arrows to form the number.

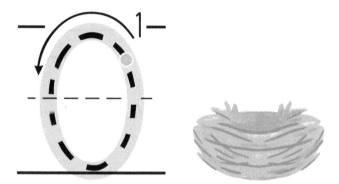

# 30. Writing 1

➡ Trace each number 1. Use the dot as the starting point and follow the arrows to form the number.

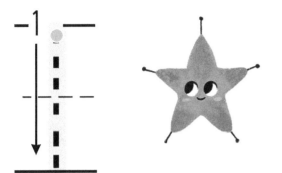

➡ Fill in the missing number.

0 _ 2 3 4 5 6 7 8 9 10

# 31. Writing 2

➡ Trace each number 2. Use the dot as the starting point and follow the arrows to form the number.

➡ Fill in the missing number.

# 32. Writing 3

➡ Trace each number 3. Use the dot as the starting point and follow the arrows to form the number.

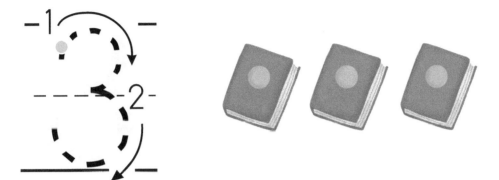

➡ Fill in the missing number.

# 33. Writing 4

➡ Trace each number 4. Use the dot as the starting point and follow the arrows to form the number.

➡ Fill in the missing number.

Skill: Fine Motor Skills

# 34. Writing 5

➡ Trace each number 5. Use the dot as the starting point and follow the arrows to form the number.

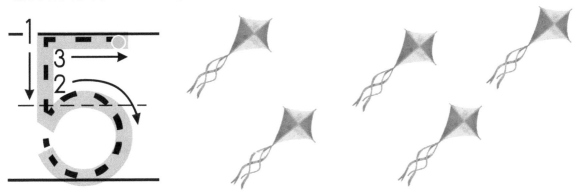

➡ Fill in the missing number.

0 1 2 3 4 _ 6 7 8 9 10

# 35. Writing 6

➡ Trace each number 6. Use the dot as the starting point and follow the arrows to form the number.

➡ Fill in the missing number.

0 1 2 3 4 5 _ 7 8 9 10

# 36. Writing 7

➡ Trace each number 7. Use the dot as the starting point and follow the arrows to form the number.

➡ Fill in the missing number.

0 1 2 3 4 5 6 _ 8 9 10

# 37. Writing 8

➡ Trace each number 8. Use the dot as the starting point and follow the arrows to form the number.

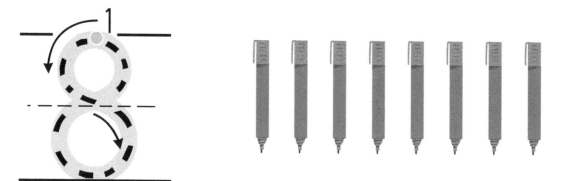

➡ Fill in the missing number.

0 1 2 3 4 5 6 7 _ 9 10

# 38. Writing 9

➡ Trace each number 9. Use the dot as the starting point and follow the arrows to form the number.

➡ Fill in the missing number.

Skill: Fine Motor Skills

# 39. Writing 10

➡ Trace each number 10. Use the dot as the starting point and follow the arrows to form the number.

➡ Fill in the missing number.

# PART 3
## Early Math Skills

# 1. Number 0

This is the number 0! Touch the number and say its name.
➡ Color all the spaces where you see the number 0. If a space does not have a 0, leave it white. What do the colored spaces show?

0 =

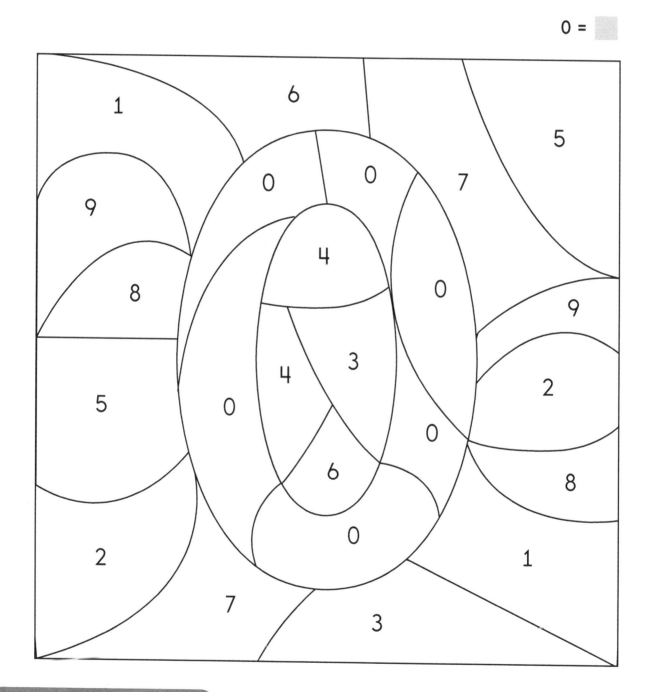

# 2. Number 1

This is the number 1! Touch the number and say its name.

➡ Point to each party hat and say the number. Circle all the party hats that have the number 1.

**Skill: Number Recognition**

# 3. Number 2

**2** This is the number 2! Touch the number and say its name.

➡ Point to each piece of candy and say the number. Draw a line from each piece of candy that has the number 2 to the candy jar.

# 4. Number 3

This is the number 3! Touch the number and say its name.
➡ Point to each balloon and say the number. Color each balloon that has the number 3.

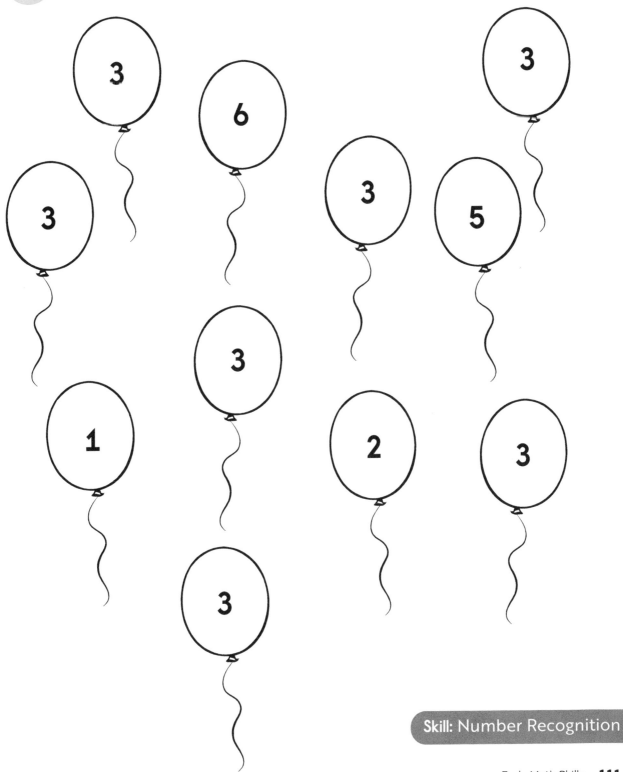

# 5. Number 4

This is the number 4! Touch the number and say its name.

➡ Help the mama duck find her 4 ducklings! Draw lines to connect the number 4's to get the mama duck to her babies.

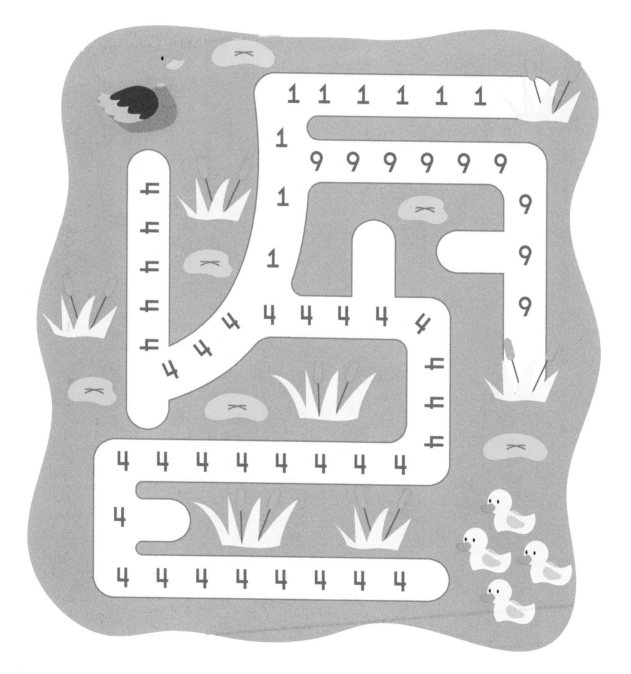

# 6. Number 5

**5**

This is the number 5! Touch the number and say its name.

➡ The 5 little monkeys have hidden all the number 5's. Find and circle each number 5 you see.

**Skill: Number Recognition**

# 7. Number 6

**6** This is the number 6! Touch the number and say its name.

➡ Color all the spaces where you see the number 6. If a space does not have a 6, leave it white. What do the colored spaces show?

6 = ▨

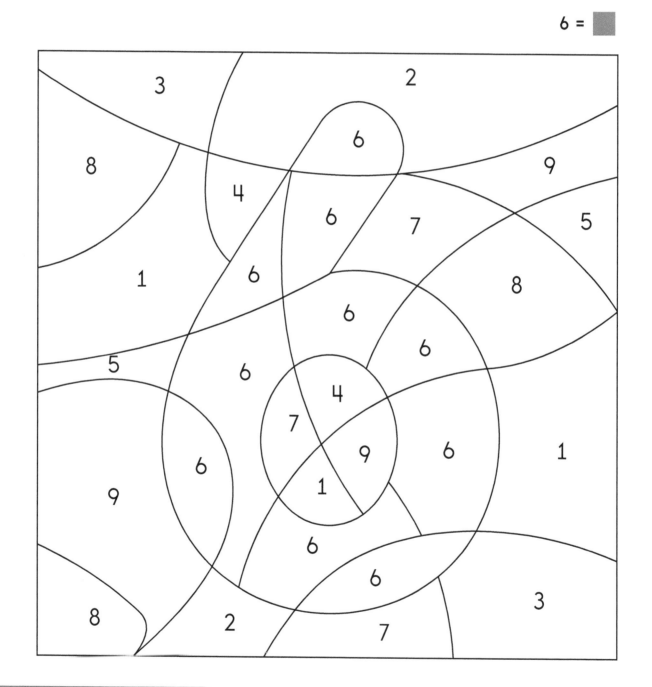

# 8. Number 7

This is the number 7! Touch the number and say its name.

➡ It's time to wash all the number 7 jerseys! Point to each jersey and say its number. If it has the number 7, draw a line from it to the washing machine.

# 9. Number 8

**8** This is the number 8! Touch the number and say its name.
➡ Point to each flower and say its number. If it has the number 8,
color the flower. If it does not have an 8, put an X on it.

9      8      8      8

8      1      8      8

**Skill: Number Recognition**

# 10. Number 9

This is the number 9! Touch the number and say its name.

➡ Help the bird find her way back to her 9 eggs! Draw lines to connect the number 9's to get the bird back to her eggs.

# 11. Number 10

10 This is the number 10! Touch the number and say its name.

➡ Point to each apple on the tree and say its number. Circle all the apples that have the number 10.

# 12. Counting 1 to 5

Counting objects tells us how many there are of something.

➡ Touch each object as you count it out loud. Draw a line from each group of objects to the matching number.

5

3

1

4

2

# 13. Counting 6 to 10

➡ Touch each object as you count it out loud. Draw a line from each group of objects to the matching number.

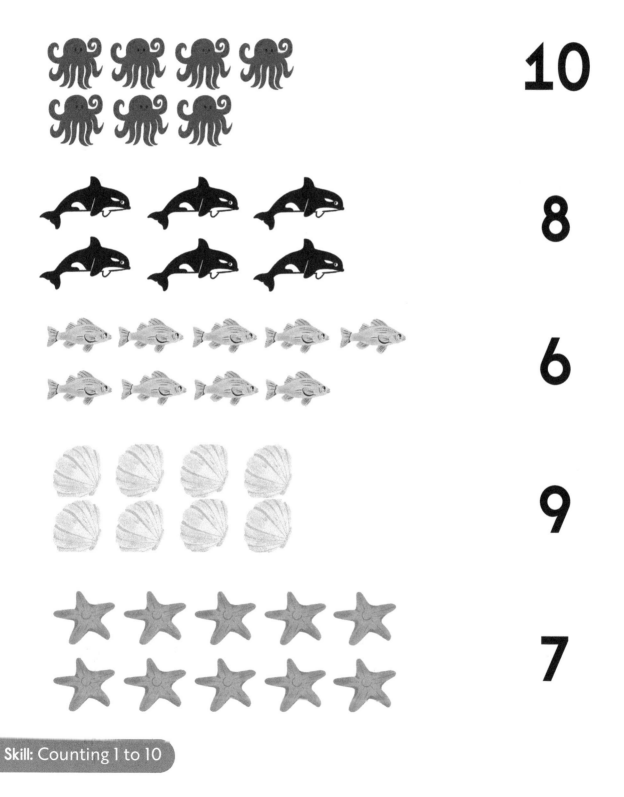

10

8

6

9

7

**Skill:** Counting 1 to 10

# 14. Spot the Shapes

There are shapes everywhere you look. Point to each shape and say its name.

➡ Can you spot the shapes in this picture? Count how many of each shape you see and write the number on the line.

Skill: Shapes

# 15. Yummy Colors

➤➤ Point to each color word and say its name. Now point to each fruit or vegetable and say its name. Color each fruit or vegetable like you would see it in real life.

Red = ▢   Yellow = ▢   Orange = ▢   Green = ▢   Blue = ▢   Purple = ▢

Apple

Banana

Green Pepper

Orange

Blueberries

Grapes

# 16. Shape Pattern

A pattern happens when objects appear over and over again in the same order.

➡ Draw a line to follow this pattern in the maze to help the princess reach her castle.

# 17. What Comes Next?

➡ Point to each picture and say its name. Circle the animal that comes next.

# 18. Make Your Own Pattern!

➡ Use 2 different colors to make a pattern on each row of shapes. Look at the first row for an example!

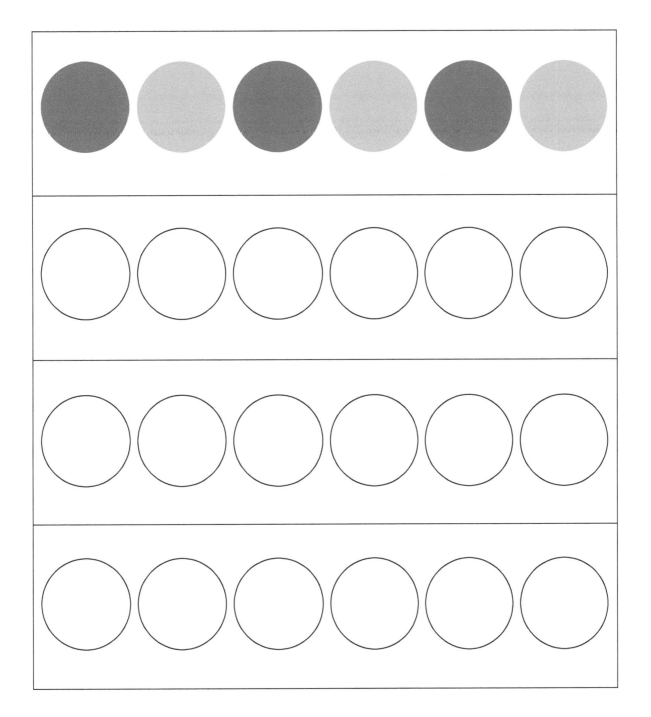

**Skill:** Patterns

# 19. Missing Fruit

➡ Point to each fruit and say the pattern. Draw the missing fruit on the blank line.

# 20. School Supplies or Lunch?

Sometimes we have to sort items so we can put them away in the correct place.

➡ Point to each item and say its name. Draw a line from the item to either the bookshelf or the refrigerator.

**Skill: Sorting and Categorization**

# 21. Odd One Out

➥ Look at the pictures in each row. Circle the picture that does not belong.

# 22. Matching Socks

➡ Color the matching socks the same color. If a sock does not have a match, put an X on it.

# 23. Animal Homes

Animals live in many different places. Some animals live in the ocean and some live in a forest.

➡ Draw a line from each place to the animals you might find there.

**Skill: Sorting and Categorization**

# 24. Animal Food

Animals eat many different types of food.

➡ Look at each animal and circle the food it likes to eat.

# 25. Make a Match

➡ Look at each item. Draw a line to match each item with something it goes with.

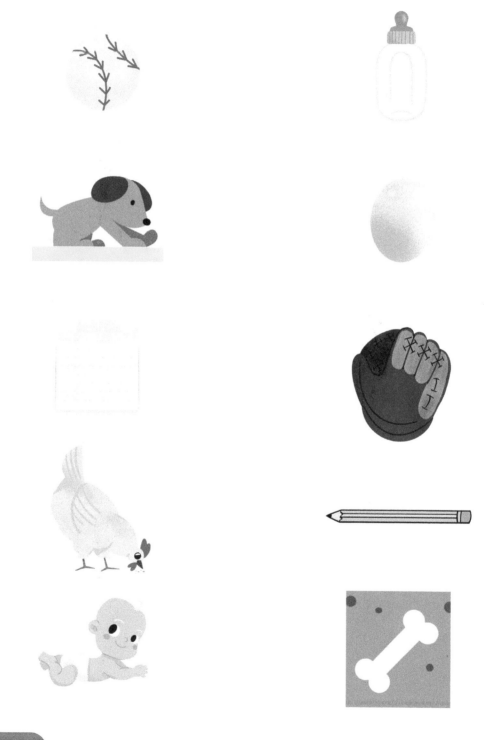

# 26. Size Them Up!

Objects come in all different sizes. When we compare sizes, we use words like smallest and biggest.

➡ Look at each row of objects. Circle the BIGGEST object. Put an X on the SMALLEST object.

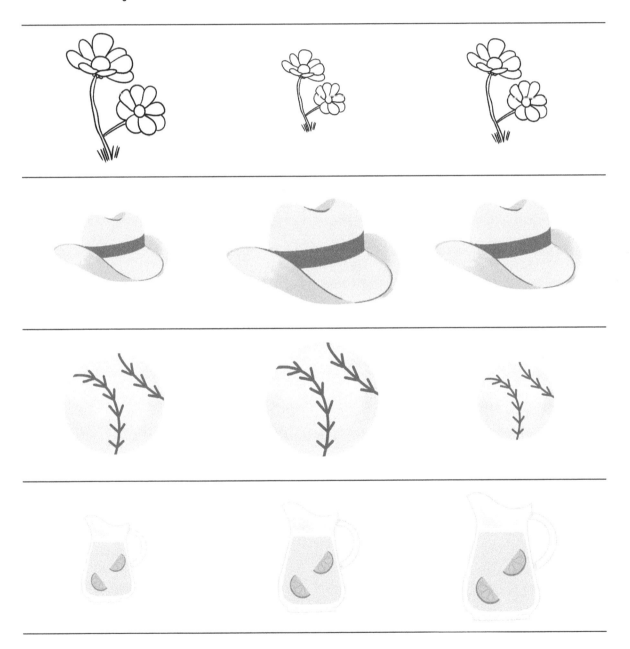

# 27. Size Match

Objects come in all different sizes. When we compare sizes, we use words like small, medium, and large.

➡ Look at each set of objects. Draw a line to match the smallest objects in each group, the medium-size objects in each group, and the largest objects in each group.

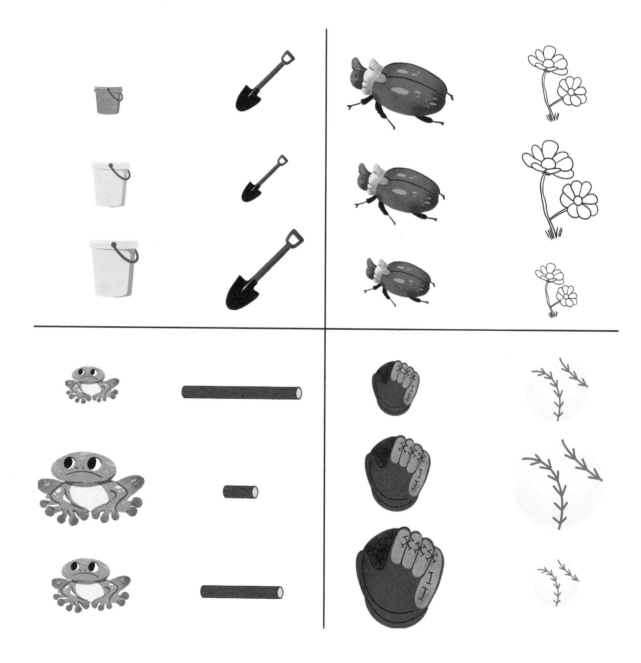

# 28. Which Holds More?

Some objects hold more of something, and some hold less.

➡ Look at each set of objects. Circle the object that holds more.

**Skill:** Measurements

# 29. Which Is Less?

When we count and compare groups of objects, the smaller number means it has less.

➡ Count each group of objects on the left. Circle one of the two groups on the right that shows less.

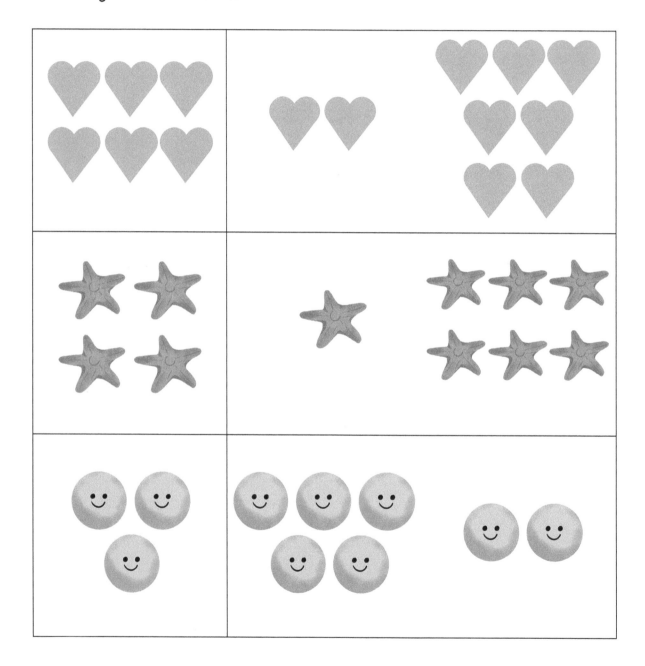

# 30. Which Is Heavier?

When we compare weight, we use words like heavier and lighter.

➡ Look at the objects in each box. Circle the object that is heavier.

# 31. Which Is Lighter?

➠ Look at each set of objects. Color the object that is lighter.

**Skill:** Weight

# Certificate of Completion

This certificate is presented to

_____

for learning skills to read, write, and do math!

▼▽▼▽▼▽▼▽▼▽▼▽▼▽▼▽▼▽▼▽

Date _____

# Answer Key

## Part 1: Pre-Reading Skills

### 1. Astronaut's Adventure

### 2. Bear's Balloons

### 3. Candy Collection

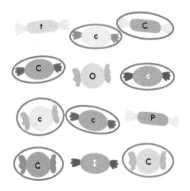

### 4. Doll Dash!

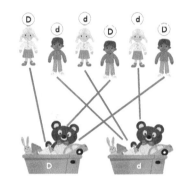

### 5. Enrique's Eggs

### 6. Fish Friends

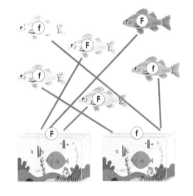

## 7. Can You Guess?

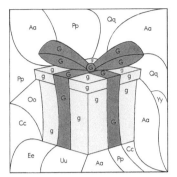

## 8. Horse Is Hungry!

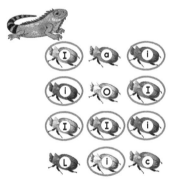

## 9. Ingrid Iguana's Insects

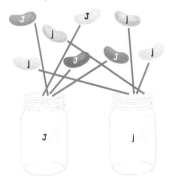

## 10. Jellybean Jars

## 11. Karl's Kites

## 12. Lion's Lemonade

## 13. Mm Mystery

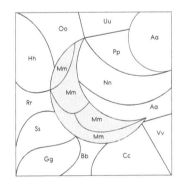

## 14. Nina's Net

### 15. Oscar the Octopus

### 16. Pepperoni Pizza

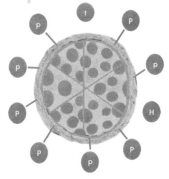

### 17. Queen's Quilt

### 18. Rainy Rr's

### 19. Silly Socks

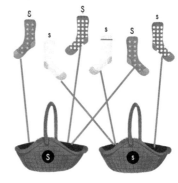

### 20. Turtle's Trail

### 21. Under the Umbrellas

6 umbrellas should be colored: 3 with U and 3 with u.

### 22. Letter Volcano

## 23. Walrus's Watermelon

| Ww | Ee | Uu | Jj | Oo | Rr | Ss |
|----|----|----|----|----|----|----|
| Ww | Qq | Zz | Cc | Rr | Ee | Ii |
| Ww | Kk | Ll | Nn | Mm | Bb | Vv |
| Ww | Ww | Ww | Yy | Aa | Tt | Cc |
| Ii | Oo | Ww | Gg | Gg | Ee | Qq |
| Dd | Ff | Ww | Ww | Ww | Ww | Yy |
| Ll | Yy | Nn | Gg | Bb | Ww | Ww |

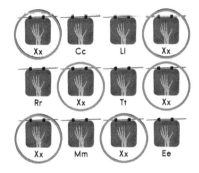

## 24. X-Ray Letters

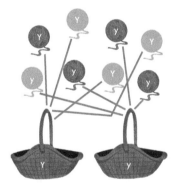

## 25. Match the Yarn

## 26. Zebra's Zoo

## 27. Make a Catch!

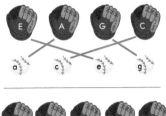

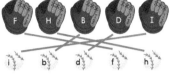

## 28. Letter Match!

Left column: M-m, Q-q, S-s, J-j, L-l

Right column: K-k, O-o, P-p, N-n, R-r

## 29. You Did It!

## 30. Aa Is for Apple

### 31. Beau's Toys

### 32. Colorful Cc's

The candy, cake, cat, car, and cow should be colored.

### 33. Dog's Bone

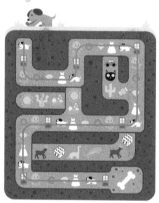

### 34. Exciting Eggs

Eggs with an elephant, elbow, eagle, ear, and eraser should be colored.

An X should be drawn on the eggs with a sun and fish.

### 35. Frog's Friends

Start with the F sound.

### 36. Gum Machine

### 37. Horses Love Hay

### 38. Ii Items

### 39. Jeep in the Jungle

### 40. Katarina's Keyboard

### 41. Lots of Ll's

### 42. Monkey's Mess

### 43. Not N!

### 44. O Is for Octopus

The ostrich, "on" light switch, ox, olive, ocean, and otter should be colored.

### 45. Pig's Produce

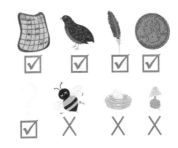

### 46. Queen's Quick Quiz

### 47. Rabbit's Race

### 48. Starry Sounds

### 49. Tons of T Words

### 50. U Is for Umbrella

The unicorn, unicycle, and umbrella should be colored.

### 51. Violet's Van

### 52. Walking Whit

### 53. Xx Examination

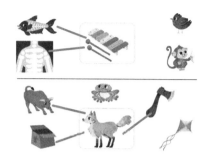

### 54. Yellow Y Words

### 55. Word Zap

The zebra, zipper, zucchini, and zigzag should be colored.

The pig, button, tomato, and clock should have an X drawn on them.

### 56. Sight Word Stars

The 3 stars with the word "play" should be colored orange.

The 3 stars with the word "we" should be colored pink.

The 3 stars with the word "see" should be colored yellow.

The 3 stars with the word "go" should be colored blue.

The 3 stars with the word "my" should be colored green.

## 57. Sweet Treats

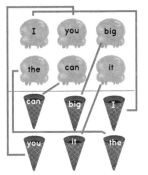

## 58. Rainy Day Words

## 59. Sight Word Sentences

I like <u>to</u> run.

We <u>are</u> here.

My mom <u>said</u> I am four.

The apple is for <u>me</u>.

## 60. Match the Opposites

## 61. Find the Opposite

## 62. Which Is Different?

## 63. Spot the Differences

## 64. Weather Wear

## Part 2: Pre-Writing Skills (no answers required)

## Part 3: Early Math Skills

### 1. Number 0

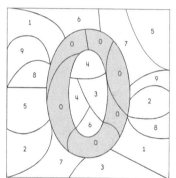

### 2. Number 1

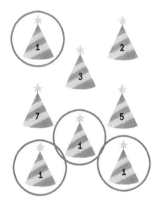

### 3. Number 2

### 4. Number 3

The 6 balloons with the number 3 should be colored.

### 5. Number 4

### 6. Number 5

7. Number 6

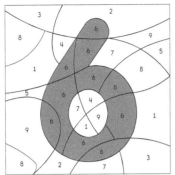

8. Number 7

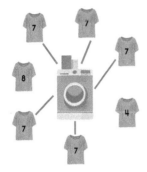

9. Number 8

The 6 flowers with the number
8 should be colored.

The 2 flowers with the numbers
9 and 1 should have an X on them.

10. Number 9

11. Number 10

12. Counting 1 to 5

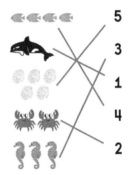

13. Counting 6 to 10

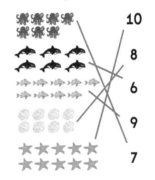

14. Spot the Shapes

## 15. Yummy Colors

apple: red

orange: orange

banana: yellow

green pepper: green

blueberries: blue

grapes: purple

## 16. Shape Pattern

## 17. What Comes Next?

1st row: monkey

2nd row: elephant

3rd row: zebra

4th row: giraffe

5th row: gorilla

## 18. Make Your Own Pattern!

Patterns will vary. (Parent: Confirm that your child has created correct patterns using two colors for each row.)

## 19. Missing Fruit

1st row: draw in grapes

2nd row: draw in a pineapple

3rd row: draw in a strawberry

4th row: draw in a watermelon

## 20. School Supplies or Lunch?

## 21. Odd One Out

1st row: circle the hat

2nd row: circle the baby

3rd row: circle the strawberry

4th row: circle the ball

## 22. Matching Socks

Sample answer (child's color choices will vary).

## 23. Animal Homes

**24. Animal Food**

monkey: circle the banana

frog: circle the insect

whale: circle the fish

**25. Make a Match**

**26. Size Them Up!**

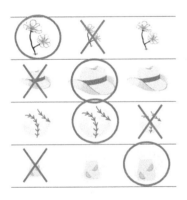

**27. Size Match**

**28. Which Holds More?**

**29. Which Is Less?**

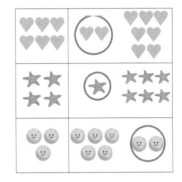

**30. Which Is Heavier?**

**31. Which Is Lighter?**

The fish, apple, bike, books, feather, and chair should be colored.

# About the Author

 **Hayley Lewallen** is the teacher and founder behind The Primary Post (ThePrimaryPost.com). She spent several years teaching kindergarten before deciding to stay home and teach her own small children. Through her website, Hayley loves creating resources and sharing fun ideas to make the lives of teachers and parents easier.